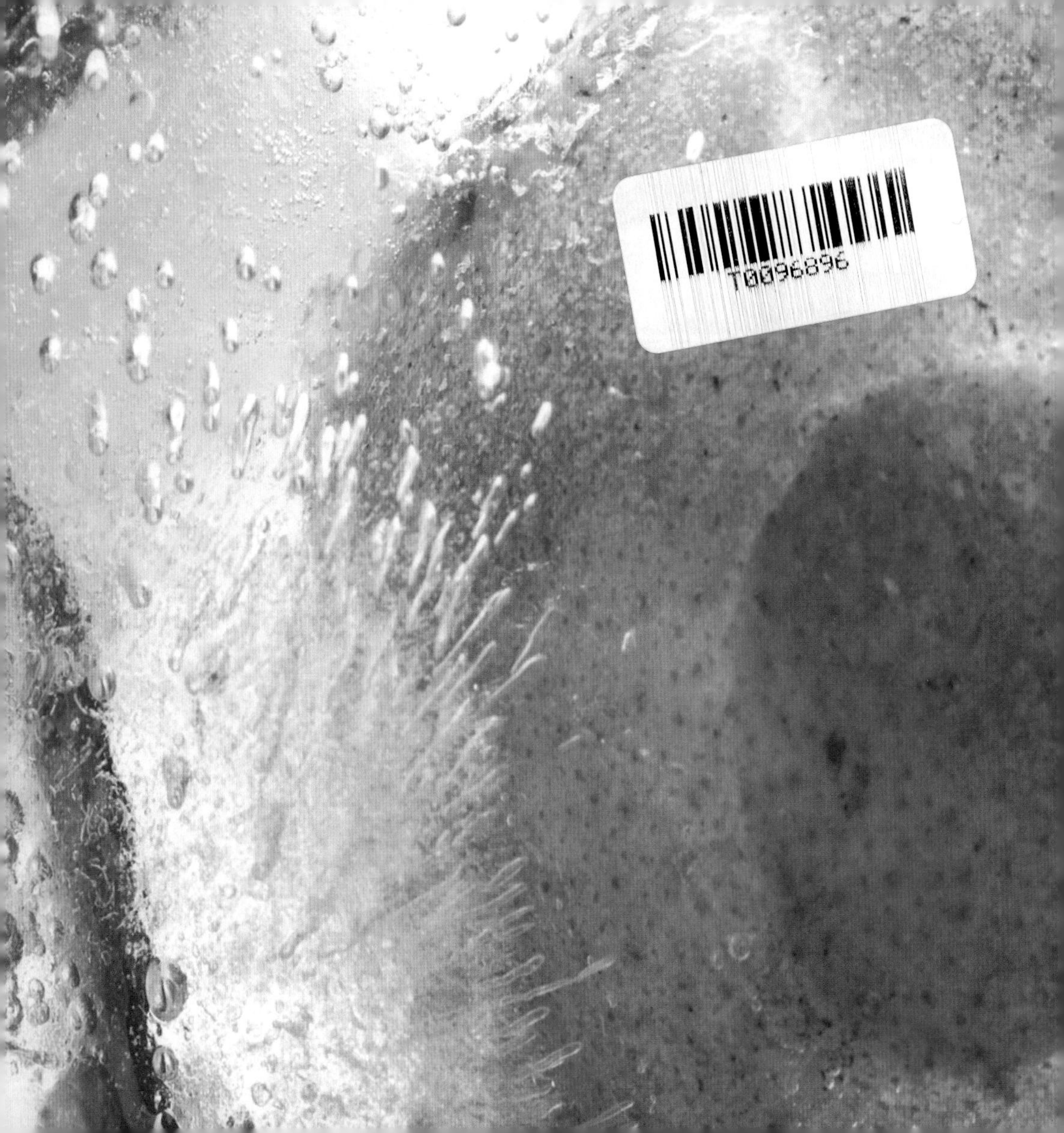
T0096896

GIN
cocktails

STUART WALTON

LORENZ BOOKS

Contents

Introduction

A bottle of gin is an indispensable standby of the drinks cupboard. In its customary guise, served with plenty of ice and a slice of lemon, the traditional gin and tonic has been a favourite tipple for over a century. However, in recent years gin production has been undergoing an exciting revolution. While the flavour of classic gin is derived principally from juniper berries, the many new artisan products are adding a host of new spice and botanical ingredients, such as apples, lavender, ginger, cassia bark, cherry blossom, roses, gooseberries and cucumber to add complexity to this enduring spirit. Gin is once again a base for elaborate cocktails, while young people have taken to drinking it on its own, and speciality gin bars are opening up all over the world.

Of the six basic spirits that are used in cocktail-making, gin is the most versatile. That may seem strange in view of its assertively perfumed character, but it is the herb and spice aromatics in its composition that enable it to blend well with a range of liqueurs and fresh fruit juices, and even other spirits. In addition to this, its colourlessness makes a neutral background for a range of flamboyant creations. Although some of the cocktails that follow have similar ingredients, to the aficionado the subtle differences in quantities of mixer, or whether shaken or stirred, make all the difference.

The classic mixer for gin is tonic water, and, just as a new era of exotic gins has taken off, companies are now producing new tonics flavoured with elderflower, lemon thyme, rosemary and ginger. Gin can, of course, rub along with plenty of other mixers such as orange juice, bitter lemon, or ginger beer. Some of the newer gins on the market are so subtle that they can be served neat: chill the bottle in the freezer and serve in small measures in shot glasses. However you take your gin, enjoy the flavour, treat it with the respect it deserves, and always drink responsibly.

Right: Plenty of ice and botanical garnishes make an attractive glass for the perfect gin and tonic.

What is gin?

Although the English often claim to be the true progenitors of gin, its origins in fact go back to 16th-century Holland. Like many other distilled drinks, it was firstly medicinal. The blend of herbs and aromatics it contained was believed to guard against a variety of ills.

Principal among these aromatics was the dark-berried plant juniper, the Dutch word for which – *genever* – is the linguistic root of the English word 'gin'.

The dark little fruits of the juniper tree contributed to the characteristic, strong perfume of gin. They are prized medicinally as a diuretic. Despite the predominance of juniper in the aroma and flavour of gin there are also other ingredients. Precise recipes vary according to the individual distiller, but other common components include angelica, liquorice, orris-root, dried citrus peel, caraway and coriander seeds, and many others.

Right: Belgravia London dry gin is distilled from 8 different fine botanicals.

It was probably British soldiers returning home from the Thirty Years War who first brought the taste for Dutch genever across the North Sea. In any case, a form of gin was being distilled in London by the 17th century, using hops and barley, and the essential juniper berries.

The rise in gin's popularity had two main causes. First, periodic hostilities with the French led to punitive tariffs on their exports and gin replaced cognac. To compound this, reform of the excise system resulted in gin becoming cheaper than beer and so it became the staple drink of the poorest classes who consumed it to excess. Gin shops were born, and public drunkenness and alcohol-related illness soared. It was only in the late Victorian period that gin began to regain a more dignified reputation, being seen as a usefully ladylike alternative to whisky and cognac.

Above: Bombay Sapphire gin is flavoured with 10 botanicals. Gordon's was established in 1769 and its recipe remains the same to this day.

How gin is made

Gin is an extremely simple drink, almost as elementary as vodka in how it is manufactured. First of all a grain spirit is produced from rye and barley, although corn is commonly used in Dutch genever and American gin. For the English style, it is ruthlessly rectified through successive distillations until all the higher alcohols are driven off. After the aromatization process, which is carried out either by macerating the dry herbs, berries and spices in the alcohol or by running the spirit through them, the finished product is bottled for immediate release.

Below: Beefeater is a famous London gin. Dutch genever is a malted grain-based gin that can only be made in Holland or Belgium.

English gin

There are two types of English gin. London dry gin is by far the more commonly known, although it doesn't have to be distilled in the capital. It is an intensely perfumed spirit, and varies greatly in quality between producers. Gordon's, Booth's and Beefeater are the most famous names. Speciality brands include Tanqueray and Bombay Sapphire, which has the distinctive pale blue bottle.

The other type is Plymouth gin, of which there is only one distiller, in Black Friars. Plymouth gin is drier than the London brands, and the aromatics give it a subtler bouquet than most gin-drinkers are used to.

Recently there has also been a steady rise in cask-aged gin, sometimes called gold gin, after the colour it leaches out of the wood. The cask-aged versions of Ableforth's Bathtub are particularly fine.

Above: Tanqueray gin was launched in 1830 in Bloomsbury, London and contains the key botanicals juniper, coriander, angelica root and liquorice.

Dutch genever

This is quite different to English gin, owing to the more pungently flavoured grain mash from which it is made. The mixture of barley, rye and corn (or maize) is often heavily malted, giving older spirits a lightly beery tinge. There are essentially two grades of genever: *oude* (old) or *jonge* (young), the latter looking more like the English article. They frequently come in an opaque 'stone' bottle, and have a more rustic flavour.

Cocktail equipment

To be a successful bartender, you will need a few essential pieces of equipment. The most vital and flamboyant is the cocktail shaker, but what you can find in the kitchen can usually stand in for the rest.

Cocktail shaker

The shaker is used for drinks that need good mixing but don't have to be crystal-clear. Once the ingredients have been thoroughly amalgamated in the presence of ice, the temperature clouds up the drink. Cocktail shakers are usually made of stainless steel, but can also be silver, hard plastic or tough glass. The Boston shaker is made of two cup-type containers that fit over each other, one normally made of glass, the other of metal. This type is often preferred by professional bartenders. For beginners, the classic three-piece shaker is easier to handle, with its base to hold the ice and liquids, a top fitted with a built-in strainer and a tight-fitting cap. Make sure you hold on to that cap while you are shaking. As a rough rule, the drink is ready when the shaker has become almost too painfully cold to hold, which is generally not more than around 15–20 seconds.

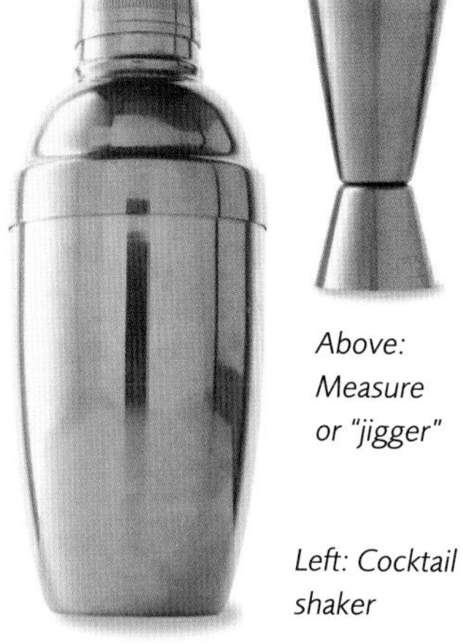

Above: Measure or "jigger"

Left: Cocktail shaker

Measure or "jigger"

Cocktail shakers usually come with a standard measure – known in American parlance as a "jigger" – for apportioning out the ingredients. This is usually a single-piece double cup, with one side a whole measure and the other a half. Once you have established the capacity of the two sides, you will save a great deal of bother.

Above: Measuring jug and spoons

Measuring jug and spoons

If you don't have a jigger, you can use a jug and/or a set of spoons for measuring out the required quantities. The measurements can be in single (25ml/1fl oz) or double (50ml/2fl oz) bar measures. Do not switch from one type of measurement to another within the same recipe.

Blender or liquidizer

Goblet blenders are the best shape for mixing cocktails that need to be aerated, as well as for creating frothy cocktails or ones made with finely crushed ice. Attempting to break up whole ice cubes in the blender may very well blunt the blades. Opt for an ice bag or dish towel, a rolling pin and plenty of brute force, or better still, use an ice crusher.

Ice bags

These plastic bags that can be filled with water and frozen are a kind of disposable ice tray. You simply press each piece of ice out of them, tearing through the plastic as you go. They also have the advantage of making more rounded pieces of ice, as opposed to the hard-angled cubes that some ice trays produce.

Ice crusher

If the prospect of breaking up ice with a hammer and dish towel comes to seem almost as much of a penance as working on a chain gang, an ice-crushing machine is the answer. It comes in two parts. You fill the top with whole ice cubes, put the lid on and, while pressing down on the top, turn the gramophone-type handle on the side. Take the top half off to retrieve the crystals of ice "snow" from the lower part. Crushed ice is used to fill the glasses for drinks that are to be served frappé. It naturally melts very quickly, though, compared to cubes.

Below: Wooden hammer and towel

Wooden hammer

Use a wooden hammer for crushing ice. The end of a wooden rolling pin works just as well.

Towel or ice bag

A towel or bag is essential for holding ice cubes when crushing, whether you are creating roughly cracked lumps or a fine snow. It must be scrupulously clean.

Ice bucket and chiller bucket

An ice bucket is useful if you are going to be making several cocktails in quick succession. They are not completely hermetic though, and ice will eventually melt in them, albeit a little more slowly than if left at room temperature. It should not be confused with a chiller bucket for bottles of champagne and white wine, which is bigger and has handles on the sides, but doesn't have a lid. A chiller bucket is intended to be filled with iced water, as opposed to ice alone.

Below: Ice crusher

Mixing pitcher or bar glass

It is useful to have a container in which to mix and stir drinks that are not shaken. The pitcher or bar glass should be large enough to hold two or three drinks. This vessel is intended for drinks that are meant to be clear, not cloudy.

Bar spoon

These long-handled spoons can reach to the bottom of the tallest tumblers and are used in jugs, or for mixing the drink directly in the glass. Some varieties of bar spoon look like a large swizzle-stick, with a long spiral-shaped handle and a disc at one end.

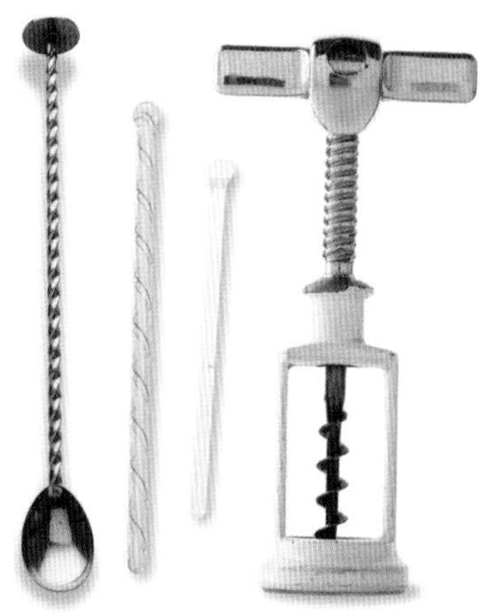

Above: Bar spoon, muddlers and corkscrew
Left: Mixing pitcher

Muddler

A long stick with a bulbous end, the muddler is used for crushing sugar or mint leaves, and so is particularly useful when creating juleps or smashes. A variety of sizes is available.

It should be used like a pestle in a mixing jug; the smaller version is for use in an individual glass. At a pinch, a flattish spoon can be used instead of a muddler, but then you will find it more awkward to apply sideways rather than downward pressure when trying to press those mint leaves.

Strainer

Used for pouring drinks from a shaker or mixing jug into a cocktail glass, the strainer's function is to remove the ice with which the drink has been prepared. Some drinks are served with the ice in (or "on the rocks") but most aren't, the reason being that you don't want the ice to unhelpfully dilute the drink. The best strainer, known professionally as a Hawthorn strainer, is made from stainless steel and looks like a flat spoon with holes and a curl of wire on the underside. It is held over the top of the glass to keep the ice and any other solid ingredients back.

Corkscrew

The fold-up type of corkscrew is known as the Waiter's Friend, and incorporates a can opener and bottle-top flipper as well as the screw itself. It is the most useful version to have to hand as it suits all purposes. The spin-handled corkscrew with a blade for cutting foil is the best one for opening fine wines.

Above: Nutmeg grater, zester and canelle knife

Sharp knife and squeezer

Citrus fruit is essential in countless cocktails. A good quality, sharp knife is required for halving the fruit, and the squeezer for extracting its juice. Although fruit juice presses are quicker to use, they are more expensive and more boring to wash up afterwards.

Nutmeg grater

A tiny grater with small holes, for grating nutmeg over frothy and creamy drinks. If this sounds a bit too fiddly, buy ready-ground nutmeg instead.

Zester and canelle knife

These are used for presenting fruit attractively to garnish glasses. If you don't already have them, don't feel obliged to run out and buy them, since drinks can look equally attractive with simply sliced fruit. The zester has a row of tiny holes that remove the top layer of skin off a citrus fruit when dragged across it (although the finest gauge on your multi-purpose grater was also designed for just this job).

A canelle knife (from the French word for a "channel" or "groove") is for making decorative stripes in the skins of a whole fruit. When sliced, they then have a groovy-looking serrated edge. It is, in effect, a narrow-gauged version of a traditional potato peeler, but is purely for decorative purposes.

Egg whisk

Use a whisk to beat a little frothy texture into egg white before you add it to the shaker. It helps the texture of the finished drink no end. An ordinary balloon whisk will do the trick, although for culinary uses, a rotary whisk with a handle (or the electric specimen) is best.

Right: Cocktail sticks and swizzle-sticks

Cocktail sticks and swizzle-sticks

Cocktail sticks are mainly decorative, used for holding ingredients such as olives that would otherwise sink to the bottom of the glass. And if you intend to eat the olive, it's handier if it's already speared, so that you don't have to commit the appalling faux pas of dipping a finger into the drink to catch it. A swizzle-stick is useful for stirring a drink, and may be substituted by food items such as a stick of celery or cucumber.

Glasses

To ensure that glasses are sparkling clean, they should always be washed and dried with a glass cloth. Although some recipes suggest chilled glasses, don't put best crystal in the freezer; leave it at the back of the refrigerator instead. An hour should be enough.

Collins glass

The tallest of the tumblers, narrow with perfectly straight sides, a Collins glass holds about 350ml/12fl oz, and is usually used for serving long drinks made with fresh juices or finished with a sparkling mixer such as soda. This glass can also stand in as the highball glass, which is traditionally slightly less tall. Uses: Tom Collins, Vunderful, Carla, and all drinks that are to be "topped up" with anything.

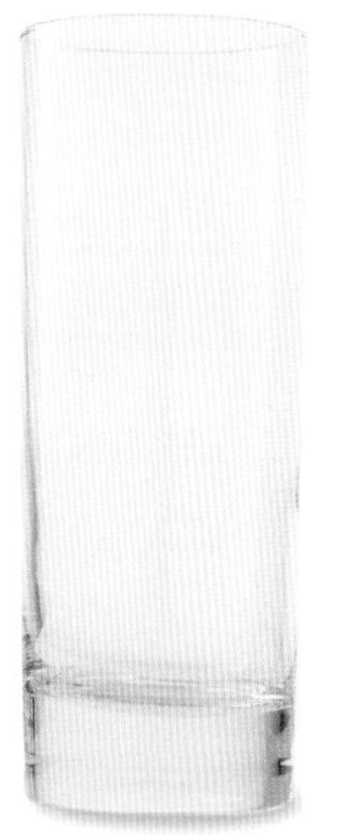

Left: Collins glass

Cocktail glass or Martini glass

This elegant glass is a wide conical bowl on a tall stem: a design that keeps cocktails cool by keeping warm hands away from the drink. It is by far the most widely used glass, so a set is essential. The design belies the fact that the capacity of this glass is relatively small (about three standard measures). Uses: The classic Martini and its variations, and almost any short, sharp, strong cocktail, including creamy ones.

Left: Cocktail glass or Martini glass

Above: Tumbler or rocks glass and liqueur glass

Tumbler or rocks glass

Classic, short whisky tumblers are used for shorter drinks, served on the rocks, and generally for drinks that are stirred rather than shaken. They should hold about 250ml/8fl oz. Uses: Bitter Gimlet, Space, Gin and It, and Damn the Weather.

Liqueur glass

Tiny liqueur glasses were traditionally used to serve small measures of unmixed drinks, and hold no more than 80ml/3fl oz. Uses: RAC, or straight gin, served ice cold.

Above: Champagne flute

Left: Large cocktail goblet

Champagne flute

This is the more acceptable glass to use for quality sparkling drinks. It is more efficient at conserving the bubbles since there is less surface area for them to break on. Always choose one with good depth, as the shorter ones look too parsimonious. Uses: Gin Crusta, and Pink Pussycat.

Large cocktail goblet

Available in various sizes and shapes, large cocktail goblets are good for serving larger frothy drinks, or drinks containing puréed fruit or coconut cream. The wider rim of this type of glass leaves plenty of room for flamboyant and colourful decorations. Uses: Blue Star, Gin Smash, Perfect Cocktail, and Gin and Lemon Fizz.

Shot glass

A tiny glass with a capacity of no more than 50ml/2fl oz, the shot glass is used for those very short, lethally strong cocktails known as shooters. If you're going to make a shooter, this is absolutely the only glass to use. No substitute will be accepted. The glass itself is usually extremely thick, as these drinks are intended to be thrown back in one, and then the glass slammed down fairly peremptorily on the bar counter. Uses: Honolulu and straight gin – go for it!

Right: Shot glass

Bartending know-how

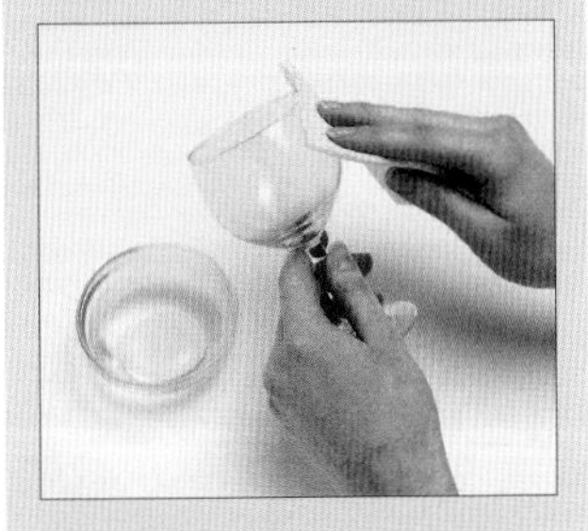

Even clean glasses should be rinsed out and wiped before use, because glasses that have been stored for any length of time can acquire a dusty taste.

Presentation is important – elegant cocktail glasses look even better when served with clean, white linen cloths.

Tricks of the trade

It is worth mastering the techniques for the preparation of good-looking drinks. The following pages give you precise directions for some of the essential procedures, such as crushing ice, as well as some not-so-essential skills, such as making decorative ice cubes. Learning these tricks of the trade is what will distinguish the dedicated bartender from the amateur dabbler.

Crushing ice

Some cocktails require cracked or crushed ice for adding to glasses, or a finely crushed ice "snow" for blending. It isn't a good idea to break ice up in a blender or food processor as you may find it damages the blades. Instead:

1 Lay out a cloth, such as a clean glass cloth or dish towel, on a work surface, and cover half of it with ice cubes. (If you wish, you can also use a cloth ice bag.)

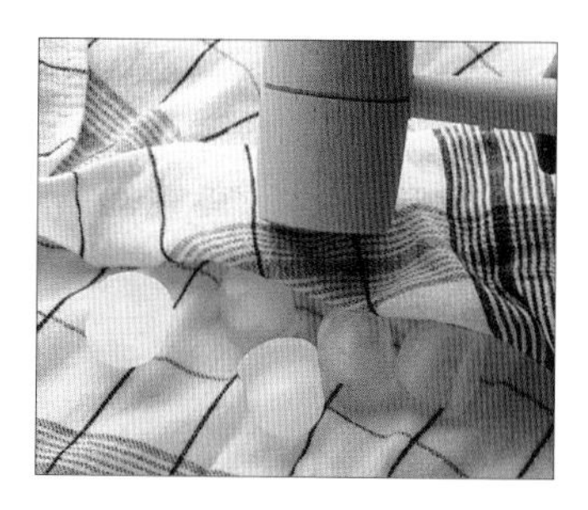

2 Fold the cloth over and, using a rolling pin or mallet, smash down on the ice firmly several times, until you achieve the required fineness.

3 Spoon the ice into glasses or a pitcher. Fine ice snow must be used immediately because it melts, but cracked or roughly crushed ice can be stored in the freezer in plastic bags.

Bartending know-how

For a moderate-sized social gathering, you may have to stay up all night with a sledgehammer. Alternatively, just buy an ice crusher.

Shaking cocktails

Cocktails that contain sugar syrups or creams require more than just a stir; they are combined and chilled with a brief shake. Remember that it is possible to shake only one or two servings at once, so you may have to work quickly in batches. Always use fresh ice each time.

1 Add four or five ice cubes to the shaker and pour in all the ingredients.

2 Put the lid on the shaker. Hold the shaker firmly in one hand, keeping the lid in place with the other hand.

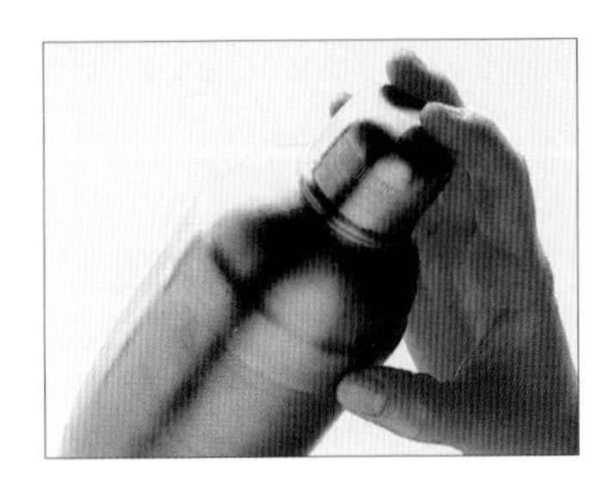

3 Shake vigorously for about 15 seconds to blend simple concoctions, and for 20–30 seconds for drinks with sugar syrups or cream. The shaker should feel extremely cold.

4 Remove the small cap and pour into the prepared glass, using a strainer if the shaker is not already fitted with one.

Bartending know-how
Never shake anything sparkling. This will flatten it.

Making decorative ice cubes

These can instantly jolly up the simplest of cocktails. Flavour and colour the water with fruit juices or bitters, and freeze in three stages.

1 Half-fill each compartment of an ice cube tray with water and place in the freezer for 2–3 hours.

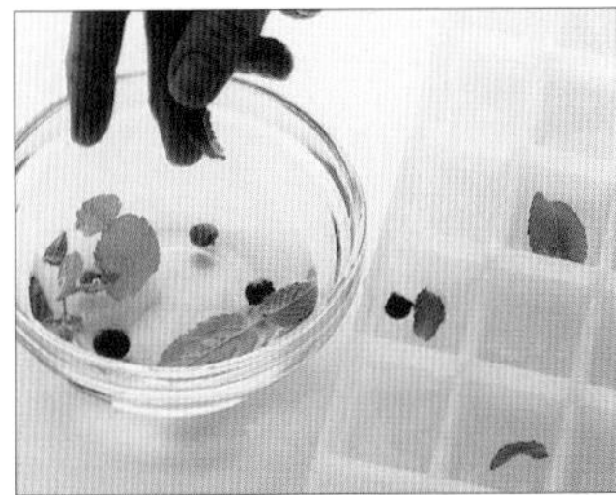

2 Prepare the fruit, olives, mint leaves, lemon rind, raisins or borage flowers and dip each briefly in water. Place in the ice-cube trays, put in the freezer and freeze again.

3 Top up the ice-cube trays with water and return to the freezer to freeze completely. Use as required, but only in one drink at each session.

Frosting glasses

The appearance and taste of a cocktail are enhanced if the rim of your glass is frosted. After frosting, place the glass in the refrigerator to chill until needed.

1 Hold the glass upside down, so the juice does not run down the glass. Rub the rim with the cut surface of a lemon, lime, orange or even a slice of fresh pineapple.

2 Keeping the glass upside down, dip the rim into a shallow layer of sugar, coconut or salt. Redip the glass, if necessary, and turn it so that the rim is well-coated.

3 Stand the glass upright and let it sit until the sugar, coconut or salt has dried on the rim, then chill.

Making twists

As an alternative to slices of the fruit, drinks can be garnished with a twist of orange, lemon or lime rind. Twists should be made before the drink itself is prepared, so that you don't keep a cold cocktail waiting. Here's how:

1 Choose a citrus fruit with an unblemished skin and a regular shape.

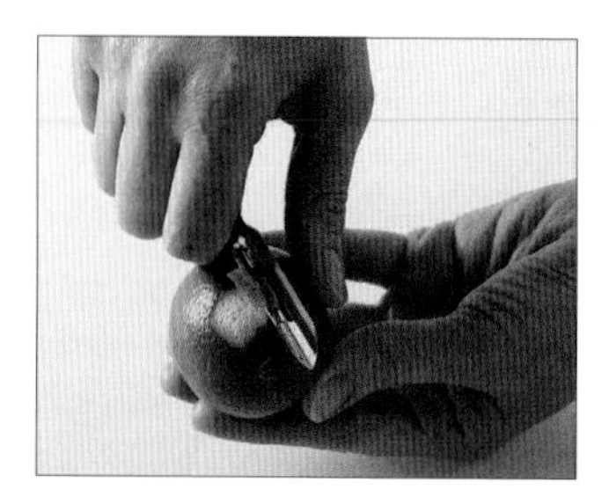

2 Using a canelle knife or potato peeler, start at the tip of the fruit and start peeling round, as though you were peeling an apple.

3 Work slowly and carefully down the fruit, being sure to keep the pared-away rind in one continuous strip.

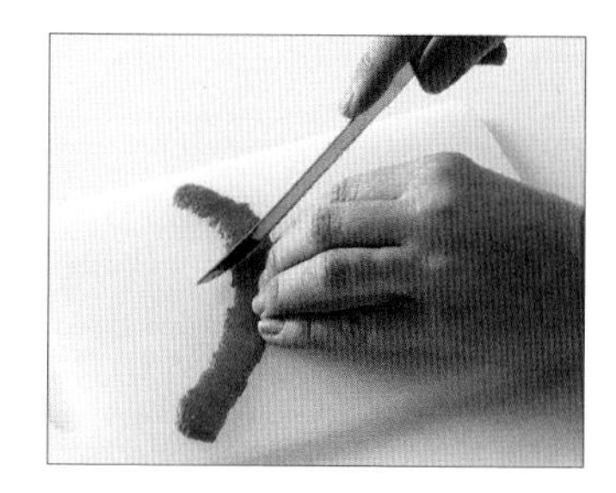

4 Trim it, if necessary, to a length that suits the glass.

5 A long twist in a cocktail glass makes the drink look sophisticated and elegant, and can be enhanced by the addition of a slice of the same fruit on the rim of the glass.

Making basic sugar syrup

A sugar syrup is sometimes preferable to dry sugar for sweetening cocktails, since it blends immediately with the other ingredients. This recipe makes about 750ml/1¼ pints.

350g/12oz sugar
600ml/1 pint water

1 Place the sugar in a heavy pan with the water, and heat gently over a low heat. Stir the mixture with a wooden spoon until all of the sugar has dissolved completely.

2 Brush the sides of the pan with a pastry brush dampened in water, to remove any sugar crystals that might cause the syrup to crystallize.

3 Bring to the boil for 3–5 minutes. Skim any scum away and when no more appears, remove the pan from the heat.

4 Cool and pour into clean, dry, airtight bottles. Keep in the refrigerator for up to one month.

Infusing gin

Steeping gin with chillies

The process of steeping gin with other flavouring agents, such as chillies, creates a whole new sensation. This recipe makes about 1 litre/1¾ pints.

25–50g/1–2oz small red chillies, or to taste, washed
1 litre/1¾ pints gin

1 Using a cocktail stick (toothpick), prick the chillies all over to release their flavours. Pack the chillies tightly into a sterilized bottle.

3 Top up with gin. Fit the cork tightly and leave in a dark place for at least ten days or up to two months.

Making sloe gin

Gin can be left to steep and absorb the flavours of ripe sloes to create a moreish liqueur. Remember to allow at least three months for it to mature – sloes picked in September will make a special Christmas drink. This recipe makes about 1.2 litres/2 pints.

450g/1lb sloes
225g/8oz sugar
1 litre/1¾ pints gin

1 Prick the tough skin of the sloes all over with a clean needle and put in a large sterilized jar. Pour in the sugar and the gin, seal tightly and shake well.

2 Store in a cool, dark cupboard and shake every other day for a week. Then shake once a week for at least two months.

3 Strain the sloe gin through muslin into a clean bowl and then pour into a sterilized bottle. Store in a cool, dark place for a further three months, if possible.

the cocktails

Tom Collins

This is similar to a Gin Fizz (see page 39), except that it isn't shaken and tends to be made with a little less soda.

2 measures/3 tbsp gin
juice of half a large lemon
5ml/1 tsp caster (superfine) sugar
soda water

Pour the gin and lemon juice into a frosted, tall glass half-filled with ice. Add the sugar and stir to dissolve. Add roughly a measure and a half of soda, a slice of lemon and a couple of straws.

Bartending know-how
For all recipes, quantites are given in metric and imperial measurements. Follow one set of measurements but not a mixture, as they are not interchangeable. 1 tsp = 5ml, 1 tbsp = 15ml. American readers should note that Club soda is referred to throughout as soda water.

Gin Sour

The Sour dates from the 1850s, and can be made with any of the basic spirits. Fresh lemon juice is naturally the key to it, with the edge taken off it by means of a pinch of sugar. However, it should never taste at all sweet, otherwise it wouldn't be worthy of its name.

2 measures/3 tbsp gin
juice of half a large lemon
5ml/1 tsp caster (superfine) sugar

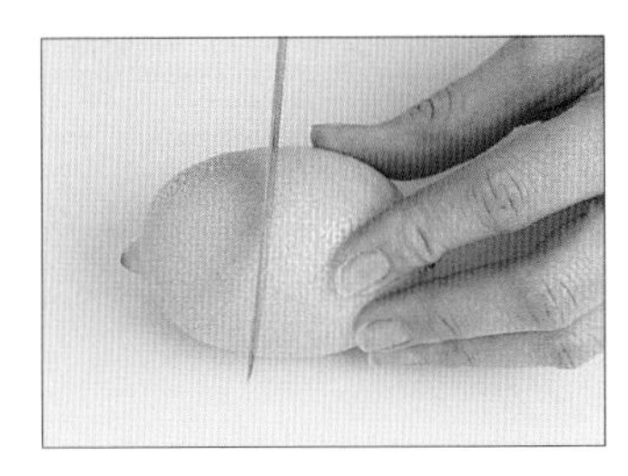

Shake all the ingredients together with ice and strain into a rocks glass or small tumbler. Some bartenders add the briefest squirt of soda just before serving for extra pep, but it is better served wholly still.

Dry Martini

No cocktail recipe is more energetically argued over than the classic dry Martini. It is basically a generous measure of virtually neat, stone-cold gin with a dash of dry white vermouth in it. But how much is a dash? Purists insist on no more than a single drop, some go for as much as half a measure of vermouth. If in doubt, it makes sense to incline towards the purist philosophy: the vermouth should be added as if it were the last bottle in existence. Inevitably, individual preference is crucial.

The drink should properly be mixed gently in a large pitcher, with ice, and then strained into the traditional cocktail glass (the real name of which is a Martini glass), which should be straight out of the freezer. A twist of lemon rind should be squeezed delicately over the surface, so that the essential oil floats on top of the drink, but don't put the lemon twist in the glass. The addition of a green olive to the glass is traditional, but disliked by some for its salty pungency.

Gibson

Well loved in Japan, this version of the Martini is named after one Charles Gibson, an American illustrator who found a cocktail onion in the drink more to his taste than the traditional olive. You can afford to be a little more generous with the vermouth.

½ measure/2 tsp dry white vermouth
2½ measures/3½ tbsp gin
2 cocktail onions

Pour the vermouth and gin into a large glass or pitcher with plenty of ice, and stir for at least 30 seconds to chill well. Strain into a Martini glass. Skewer the onions on to the end of a cocktail stick and add to the glass, so that they sit temptingly at the bottom. Better still, pour out the drink over the onions to release their flavours.

Gin Swizzle

The Gin Swizzle dates from the early 19th century, and was originally a drink made frothy by plenty of energetic stirring. The implement used for this, the swizzle-stick, took its name from the drink.

2 measures/3 tbsp gin
¼ measure/1 tsp sugar syrup
juice of a lime
2 dashes Angostura bitters (see page 24)

Beat all the ingredients together (as if you were preparing eggs for an omelette) in a large jug, with ice. When the drink is good and foaming, strain it into a tall glass. Alternatively, make the drink in the tall glass, but remember to stir it up vigorously with a swizzle-stick. Some recipes add soda water to achieve the swizzle effect, but originally it was all done by elbow grease. The froth will subside fairly quickly anyway.

Blue Star

The unearthly colour produced by mixing blue and orange in this drink is further enhanced by serving it frappé, over plenty of crushed ice.

1 measure/1½ tbsp gin
¾ measure/3 tsp Noilly Prat or other dry vermouth
⅓ measure/1½ tsp blue curaçao
1 measure/1½ tbsp orange juice

Shake all the ingredients well with ice, and strain into a cocktail glass full of finely crushed ice. Garnish with a half-slice of orange.

Bartending know-how
A 'dash' is the amount that escapes from the bottle by tilting it and righting it again over the shaker in about half a second.

Cloister

A strong lemony, herbal flavour pervades the Cloister. It is a short drink that delivers a strong kick-start to the tastebuds.

1½ measures/6 tsp gin
½ measure/2 tsp yellow Chartreuse
½ measure/2 tsp grapefruit juice
¼ measure/1 tsp lemon juice
¼ measure/1 tsp sugar syrup

Shake all the ingredients well with ice, and strain into a cocktail glass. Garnish with a twist of grapefruit rind, draped over the glass rim.

Bartending know-how
The invention of gin is wrongly credited to one Franz de le Boë, a medical professor at Leiden University in the Netherlands, in the mid-17th century, but it is much older than that.

Wilga Hill Boomerang

This sundowner is mixed in a large pitcher half-filled with ice cubes, and is served whilst still extremely cold.

1 measure/1½ tbsp gin
¼ measure/1 tsp dry vermouth
¼ measure/1 tsp sweet red vermouth
1 measure/1½ tbsp apple juice
dash Angostura bitters
2 dashes maraschino cherry juice

Pour the gin, dry and sweet vermouths and apple juice into a pitcher half-filled with cracked ice, and stir until the outside of the glass has frosted. Add the Angostura bitters and cherry juice to the bottom of a cocktail glass and add crushed ice, and then strain in the mixed cocktail. Prepare a strip of orange rind and a maraschino cherry to decorate the glass.

Gin Smash

Try this cocktail with any fresh mint you can find: peppermint and spearmint would each contribute their own flavour to this simple and very refreshing summery drink.

15ml/1 tbsp caster (superfine) sugar
4 sprigs fresh mint
2 measures/3 tbsp gin

Dissolve the sugar in a little water in the cocktail shaker. Add the mint and, using a muddler, bruise and press the juices out of the leaves. Then add plenty of crushed ice, and finally the gin. Shake for about 20 seconds. Strain into a small wine glass filled with crushed ice. If desired, add fresh mint sprigs and drinking straws.

Carla

This fruity concoction owes its character to Dutch genever, which should be used in preference to London gin.

1½ measures/6 tsp jonge genever
2 measures/3 tbsp orange juice
1 measure/1½ tbsp passion fruit juice
2 measures/3 tbsp lemonade

Shake the first three ingredients together with a couple of handfuls of crushed ice, and pour, unstrained, into a highball glass. Add the lemonade. You could garnish with a slice of orange.

Bartending know-how
In the Netherlands, genever is nearly always drunk neat, accompanied by a chaser of the local beer.

Bennett

Dating from the 1920s, this short drink is sometimes seen spelt with only one "t", and with a small quantity of sugar syrup added to it, but this is the original formula, which has a sharper edge.

1½ measures/6 tsp gin
½ measure/2 tsp lime juice
2 dashes Angostura bitters

Shake well with ice and strain into a cocktail glass.

Pink Pussycat

An object-lesson in how easily gin takes to a range of tangy fruit flavours in a mixed drink, Pink Pussycat also has – as its name suggests – a most beguiling colour.

2 measures/3 tbsp gin
3 measures/4½ tbsp pineapple juice
2 measures/3 tbsp grapefruit juice
½ measure/2 tsp grenadine

Shake all the ingredients well with ice, and strain into a champagne flute. Garnish with a segment of grapefruit.

Gin Crusta

Prepare the glass in advance and keep it chilled in the refrigerator ready for instant use. The depth of pink colour will depend on the strength of the maraschino cherry juice you use.

1 lemon
25g/2 tbsp golden brown sugar
3 dashes sugar syrup
2 dashes maraschino cherry juice
2 dashes Angostura bitters
1 measure/1½ tbsp gin

Cut both ends off the lemon and, using a canelle knife, peel it thinly in one long, continuous piece. Halve the lemon and rub the rim of a glass with the cut surface. Dip it into the sugar to create a decorative rim. Arrange the lemon rind in a scroll on the inside of a high-sided glass. Add the sugar syrup, cherry juice, Angostura, gin and juice of a quarter of the lemon to a cocktail shaker, half-filled with ice. Shake well and strain into the prepared glass.

Vunderful

A long, lazy Sunday afternoon tipple, conjured up in the heat of southern Africa. This recipe contains 20 servings.

400g/14oz can lychees
2 peaches, sliced
¾ bottle gin

For each serving you will need:
1 measure/1½ tbsp Pimm's
2–3 dashes Angostura bitters
5 measures/120ml/4fl oz chilled tonic water or lemonade

Strain the lychees from the syrup and place them in a jar with the peach slices and the gin. Let them sit overnight or for anything up to a month. For each serving, mix in a large pitcher a measure of the lychee gin with the Pimm's and the bitters to taste. Strain into tall tumblers filled with ice cubes. Add chilled tonic water or lemonade to top up. Put a couple of the drained gin-soaked lychees and peach slices into each glass and add a half-slice of lime to the glass rim.

Luigi

A 1920s classic, Luigi was created at the Criterion restaurant on London's Piccadilly Circus by one Luigi Naintre.

1½ measures/6 tsp gin
1½ measures/6 tsp dry vermouth
¼ measure/1 tsp grenadine
dash Cointreau
juice of half a tangerine or mandarin orange

Shake well with ice and strain into a glass. Add a segment of tangerine.

Monkey Gland

From the classic cocktail era of the early 1920s, this drink was created at Ciro's Club in London, a legendary jazz nightspot just off the Charing Cross Road. Head bartender Harry McElhone later moved to Paris to run Harry's New York Bar, where he ascended to true international renown.

2 measures/3 tbsp gin
1 measure/1½ tbsp orange juice
½ measure/2 tsp grenadine
½ measure/2 tsp absinthe

Shake the ingredients with plenty of ice, and strain into a large wine glass. Garnish with a slice of orange.

My Fair Lady

This frothy, fruity cocktail was invented at London's Savoy Hotel in the 1950s to coincide with a production of the much-loved Lerner and Loewe musical based on George Bernard Shaw's play *Pygmalion*.

1 measure/1½ tbsp gin
½ measure/2 tsp orange juice
½ measure/2 tsp lemon juice
¼ measure/1 tsp crème de fraise
1 egg white

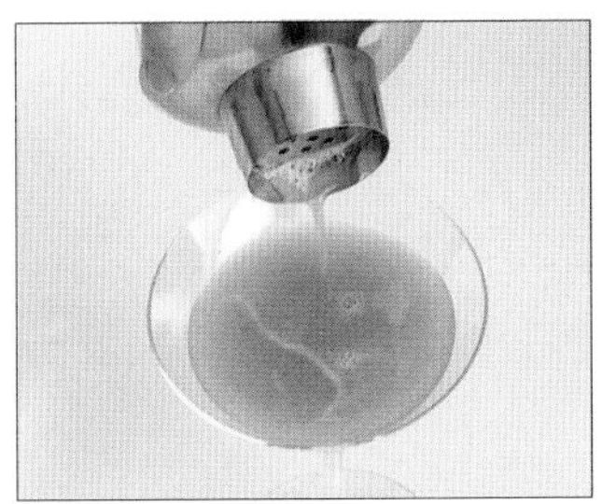

Shake all the ingredients thoroughly with ice, and strain into a cocktail glass. Garnish with a slice of orange.

White Lady

This is one of the classic cocktail recipes of the 1920s, and is still going strong today. The high strength of the alcohol ingredients and the sharpness of the lemon quite belie its innocuous reputation as a "lady's drink".

1 measure/1½ tbsp gin
1 measure/1½ tbsp Cointreau
1 measure/1½ tbsp lemon juice

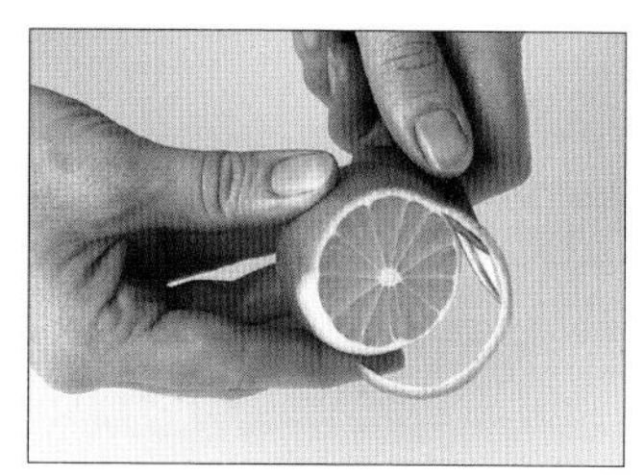

Shake the ingredients with ice and strain into a frosted cocktail glass. Some recipes also add 5ml/1 tsp egg white. The *Savoy Cocktail Book* makes no mention of it. It simply gives the drink a frothier texture, if that's what you like. Garnish with a lime twist.

Pink Lady

Yet another of the "Ladies", this one is more venerable than most. It dates from before the First World War, and was named after a now forgotten hit stage play. The pink colour is achieved by means of a relatively large quantity of the pomegranate syrup, grenadine.

caster (superfine) sugar, for frosting
1½ measures/6 tsp Plymouth gin
½ measure/2 tsp grenadine, plus extra for frosting
½ measure/2 tsp double (heavy) cream
¼ measure/1 tsp lemon juice
1 measure/1½ tbsp egg white

Dip the rim of a champagne saucer or bowl-shaped cocktail glass into grenadine and then into caster sugar to create a bright pink, frosted rim. Shake the cocktail ingredients with ice and strain into the prepared glass. Garnish with a glacé cherry.

Gin and Lemon Fizz

If gin and tonic is your tipple, try this chilled alternative. The fruit and flower ice cubes make a lively decoration for any iced drink. This recipe serves two.

mixture of small edible berries or currants
pieces of thinly pared lemon or orange rind
tiny edible flowers
4 scoops of lemon sorbet
30ml/2 tbsp gin
120ml/4fl oz chilled tonic water

To make the decorated ice cubes, place each fruit, piece of rind or flower in a section of an ice-cube tray. Carefully fill with water and freeze for several hours until the cubes are solid.

Divide the sorbet into two cocktail glasses or use small tumblers, with a capacity of about 150ml/¼ pint. Spoon over the gin and add a couple of the ornamental ice cubes to each glass. Top up with tonic water and serve immediately.

Bijou

This recipe dates from the 1920s. The mix of Chartreuse and vermouth does indeed create a rather jewel-like colour. It must be Plymouth gin, by the way.

1 measure/1½ tbsp Plymouth gin
1 measure/1½ tbsp green Chartreuse
1 measure/1½ tbsp sweet red vermouth
dash orange bitters (or curaçao)

Stir all the ingredients well with ice in a pitcher, and then strain into a cocktail glass. Squeeze a twist of lemon over the drink, drop it in and add a cherry.

Merry Widow

This is another 1920s recipe, this time at the bone-dry end of the spectrum, notwithstanding that splash of Bénédictine. It's a strong one too, all alcohol, which explains the merriness of the widow.

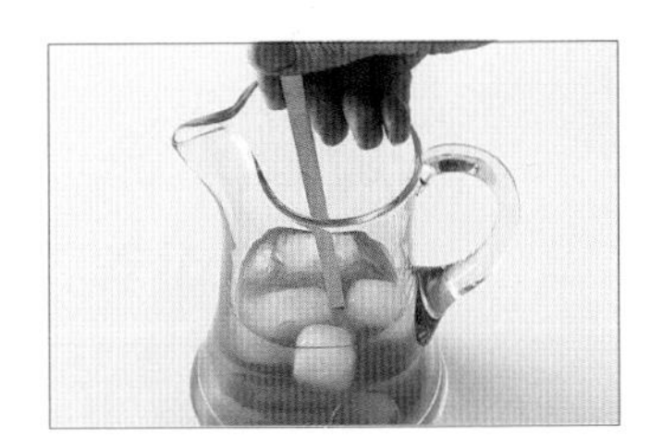

1 measure/1½ tbsp gin
1 measure/1½ tbsp dry vermouth
2 dashes absinthe
2 dashes Bénédictine
2 dashes Angostura bitters

Stir all the ingredients well with ice in a pitcher, and then strain into a large wine glass. Squeeze a twist of lemon rind over the drink, and then drop it in.

Bronx

An utterly satisfying mixture of gin and both vermouths, Bronx is basically a sort of gin Manhattan with a little orange juice. It is a New York cocktail that dates back to the early years of the 20th century. Like all such mixtures, it makes a very effective aperitif.

1½ measures/6 tsp gin
¾ measure/3 tsp dry vermouth
¾ measure/3 tsp sweet red vermouth
juice of a quarter of an orange

Shake all the ingredients well with ice, and strain into a cocktail glass. Garnish with a half-slice of orange.

Barbarella

This is a colourful drink named after the title character in the classic sci-fi movie, played by Jane Fonda.

1 measure/1½ tbsp Plymouth gin
1 measure/1½ tbsp dry vermouth
½ measure/2 tsp Galliano
¼ measure/1 tsp blue curaçao
2 measures/3 tbsp sparkling bitter lemon

Shake the first four ingredients well with ice, and strain into a rocks glass that has been half-filled with cracked ice. Add the bitter lemon, and garnish with a slice of lemon.

Gin Fizz

The combination of sourness and fizziness in this 19th-century recipe is what makes it so refreshing.

2 measures/3 tbsp gin
juice of half a large lemon
5ml/1 tsp caster (superfine) sugar
soda water

Shake the gin, lemon juice and sugar with ice until the sugar is properly dissolved. Pour out into a frosted, tall, narrow glass half-filled with ice, and top up with soda. Add two straws. There should ideally be a little less soda than the other combined ingredients, but it is very much a matter of personal taste.

Bartending know-how
It is estimated that, at the time the Gin Act was introduced in 1736, average consumption in London had hit something like two-thirds of a bottle per head per day.

Red Cloud

Although red clouds at night were once said to be a sailor's delight, you don't have to be ocean-bound to enjoy one of these.

1½ measures/6 tsp gin
¾ measure/3 tsp apricot brandy
½ measure/2 tsp lemon juice
¼ measure/1 tsp grenadine
dash Angostura bitters

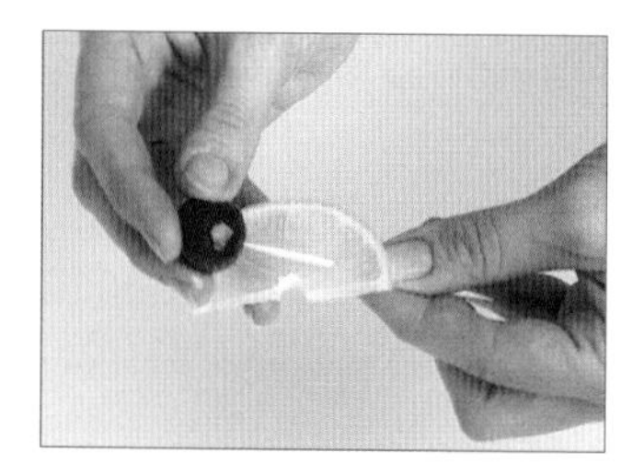

Shake all the ingredients well with ice, and strain into a champagne saucer or cocktail glass. Garnish with a half-slice of lemon and a fresh cherry.

Maiden's Blush

There were two quite distinct recipes for Maiden's Blush, even in the 1920s. The first mixed gin with orange curaçao, lemon juice and grenadine. This one was a slightly more lethal proposition, and the blush effect in the colour is more apparent, if you need any excuse to up the ante.

2 measures/3 tbsp gin
1 measure/1½ tbsp absinthe
¼ measure/1 tsp grenadine

Shake all the ingredients well with ice, and strain into an ice-cold cocktail glass.

Tangier

An intercontinental flight on this page starts in Morocco with this sweetly orangey number. The choice of city for the name distantly reflects the tangerines that go into Mandarine Napoléon.

1 measure/1½ tbsp gin
1 measure/1½ tbsp Cointreau
1 measure/1½ tbsp Mandarine Napoléon

Shake all the ingredients well with ice, and strain into a cocktail glass. Decorate the glass with a spiral twist of orange rind, wrapped around a cocktail stick.

Honolulu

This fruity little shooter should be served in a shot glass.

1 measure/1½ tbsp gin
¼ measure/1 tsp pineapple juice
¼ measure/1 tsp orange juice
¼ measure/1 tsp lemon juice
¼ measure/1 tsp pineapple syrup (from a can)
1 drop Angostura bitters

Shake all but the last ingredient with ice and strain into a shot glass. Add a single drop of Angostura to the drink, and knock back in one.

Perfect Cocktail

Another gin and vermouth recipe from the 1920s, this is a little like Bronx, but without the orange juice. Then again, substitute Pernod for the gin and you have a Duchess.

1 measure/1½ tbsp gin
1 measure/1½ tbsp dry vermouth
1 measure/1½ tbsp sweet red vermouth

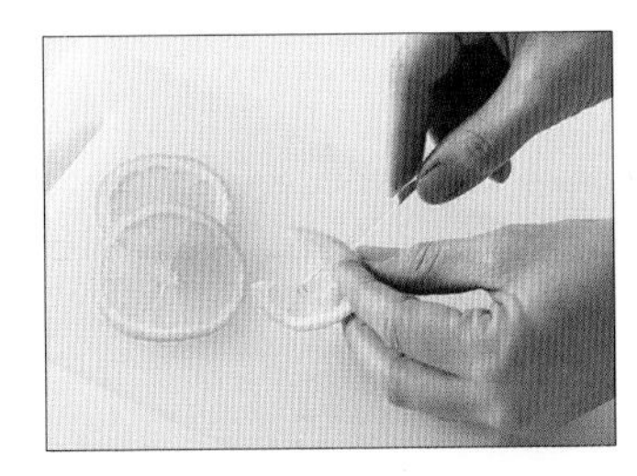

Shake all the ingredients well with ice, and strain into a cocktail glass. Garnish with a twist of lemon rind.

Dundee

What else but classic Scottish ingredients (two of them, in fact) could give a drink a name like this? This is a dry, sour cocktail with quite a kick.

1 measure/1½ tbsp gin
¾ measure/3 tsp Scotch
½ measure/2 tsp Drambuie
½ measure/2 tsp lemon juice

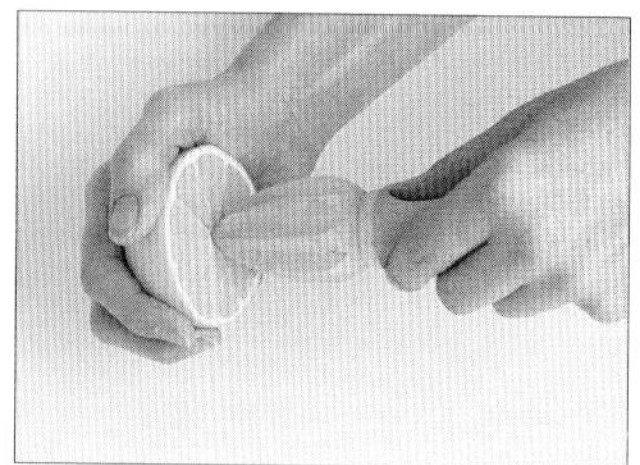

Shake all the ingredients well with ice, and strain into a whisky tumbler. Squeeze a twist of lemon rind over the drink, and then drop it into the glass.

Whiteout

A highly indulgent preparation which looks irresistible. It is a sweet, chocolate cream cocktail that tastes far more innocuous than it actually is.

1½ measures/6 tsp gin
1 measure/1½ tbsp white crème de cacao
1 measure/1½ tbsp double (heavy) cream

Shake all the ingredients very well with ice to amalgamate the cream fully, and then strain into a chilled cocktail glass. Grate a small piece of white chocolate over the surface.

Juan-les-Pins

Once the preferred destination of the Mediterranean jet-set, the Riviera resort is fittingly honoured by this appetizing mixture of gin, an aperitif and a liqueur.

1 measure/1½ tbsp gin
¾ measure/3 tsp white Dubonnet
½ measure/2 tsp apricot brandy
dash lemon juice

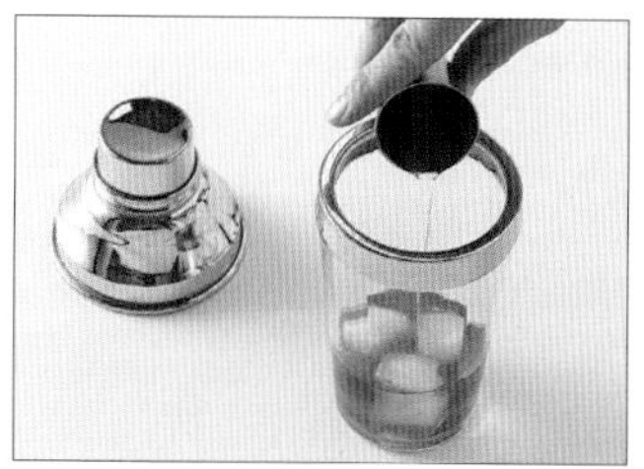

Shake all the ingredients well with ice, and strain into a cocktail glass. Garnish with a slice of apricot and a cherry speared by a cocktail stick.

Negroni

The Negroni is an Americano with gin, making an altogether drier drink. It is named after one Count Camillo Negroni who invented this formula at a bar in Florence, Italy, just after the First World War. The addition of gin elevates the drink into a different class altogether. It makes a particularly brilliant aperitif.

2 measures/3 tbsp gin
1 measure/1½ tbsp sweet red vermouth
¾ measure/3 tsp Campari

Mix the three ingredients in a tumbler with ice. Squeeze a twist of orange rind over the drink and then drop it in. NB: a twist of lemon is completely unacceptable.

Matinée

In this nourishing, creamy, eggy mixture, the relatively small amount of Sambuca shines forth. Whip up the egg white a little before adding it to the shaker.

1 measure/1½ tbsp gin
½ measure/2 tsp Sambuca
½ measure/2 tsp double (heavy) cream
½ egg white
dash lime juice

Shake all the ingredients well with plenty of ice, and strain into a chilled cocktail glass. Sprinkle with finely grated nutmeg.

Bartending know-how
When three coffee beans are taken in a flaming Sambuca, they represent health, wealth and happiness.

Singapore Sling

One of the all-time greats, Singapore Sling was created in 1915 at the world-famous Raffles Hotel in Singapore. Some recipes omit the soda for a slightly stronger drink. Some add a dash of grenadine just to deepen the pink colour, but it should nonetheless be no more than a fairly delicate blush.

2 measures/3 tbsp gin
⅔ measure/1 tbsp cherry brandy
⅔ measure/1 tbsp Cointreau
juice of 1 lemon
5ml/1 tsp caster (superfine) sugar
3 measures/4½ tbsp soda water

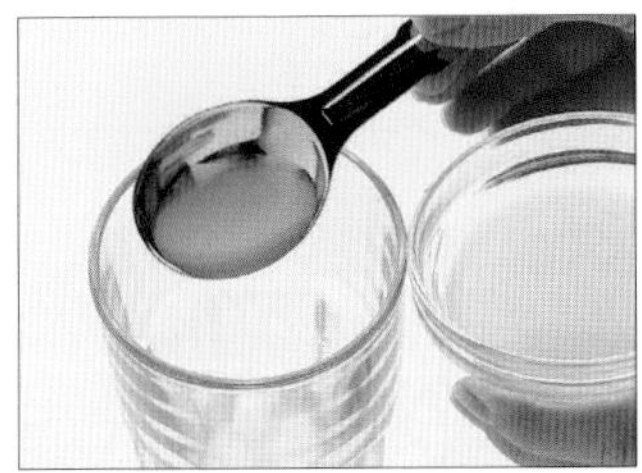

Shake all but the soda well with ice, and strain into a highball glass. Add the soda, and decorate with a twist of lemon and a black cherry pierced with two cocktail sticks.

RAC

This was created on the eve of the First World War by the barman of the Royal Automobile Club in London's Pall Mall.

1½ measures/6 tsp gin
¾ measure/3 tsp dry vermouth
¾ measure/3 tsp sweet red vermouth
¼ measure/1 tsp orange bitters

Shake well with ice, and strain into a glass. Squeeze a twist of orange rind over the top to release its oil.

Damn the Weather

This cocktail has been around since the 1920s, and presumably commemorates a particularly persistent gloomy spell.

1 measure/1½ tbsp gin
½ measure/2 tsp sweet red vermouth
½ measure/2 tsp orange juice
¼ measure/1 tsp orange curaçao

Shake well with ice, and strain into a chilled whisky tumbler. Add a twist of orange wrapped around a cocktail stick.

Bartending know-how
First invented by the Dutch, Curaçao was a white, rum-based liqueur flavoured with the peel of bitter green oranges found by the settlers on the Caribbean island of the same name. It comes in a range of colours; the orange Curaçao is a deep, burnished tawny orange.

Silver Jubilee

This was created for Queen Elizabeth's Silver Jubilee in 1977. There is a tendency now to up the gin quotient to as much as double this quantity, but I find that these proportions work perfectly well.

1 measure/1½ tbsp gin
1 measure/1½ tbsp crème de banane
1 measure/1½ tbsp double (heavy) cream

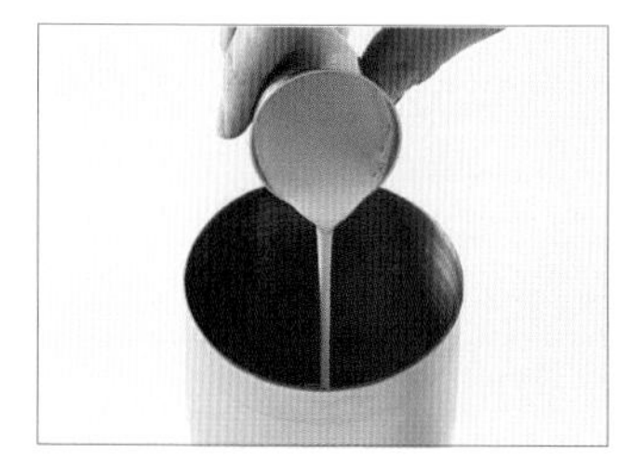

Shake all the ingredients thoroughly with ice to amalgamate the cream, and strain into a chilled cocktail glass. Grate a little dark chocolate over the surface, if desired.

Caruso

Towards the end of his life, the celebrated Italian opera singer Enrico Caruso stayed at the Hotel Sevilla in Cuba, where an obliging barman created this cocktail in his honour.

1 measure/1½ tbsp gin
1 measure/1½ tbsp dry vermouth
1 measure/1½ tbsp green crème de menthe

Shake well with ice and strain into a cocktail glass. Some versions these days use a little less crème de menthe than a whole measure, as the flavour is so strong, but this is the original recipe.

Angel Face

To be dedicated to the one you love, perhaps, although after a couple of these, almost anyone will start to look good. It's another all-alcohol mix, and a pretty dry and bracing one at that, although the liqueur contributes a touch of almondy sweetness to the finish.

1 measure/1½ tbsp gin
1 measure/1½ tbsp apricot brandy
1 measure/1½ tbsp calvados

Shake all the ingredients well with ice, and strain into a cocktail glass. Garnish with a half-slice of lemon.

Leap Year

The particular year in question was 1928, when Harry Craddock, a barman at the Savoy Hotel in London, created this drink for a party held there on February 29.

2 measures/3 tbsp gin
½ measure/2 tsp Grand Marnier
½ measure/2 tsp sweet red vermouth
dash lemon juice, plus lemon rind

Shake well and strain into a cocktail glass. Squeeze a bit of lemon rind over the surface of the drink so that a little of its oil sprays out.

Bartending know-how
Vermouth comes in a variety of styles. The red is made with red wine; the dry white gains an amber tinge from ageing in oak casks; bianco is sweetened-up dry white; the pink version is based on rosé wine.

Golf

This is an old 1920s recipe for a very short drink that is a distant relation of the Martini. It was indeed originally known as the Golf Martini, but is clearly for those who like a little more vermouth with their gin.

1 measure/1½ tbsp gin
½ measure/2 tsp dry vermouth
2 dashes Angostura bitters

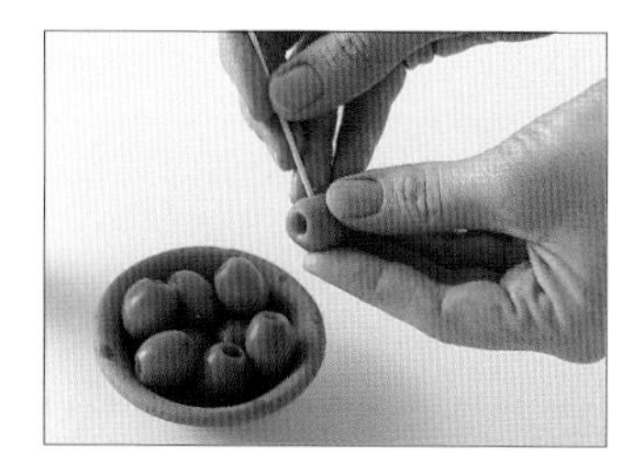

Stir all the ingredients well with ice in a small pitcher, and strain into a tumbler. Garnish with a green olive.

Gin and It

The name of this drink is a shortened form of gin and Italian, so-called in the days when Italian vermouths were inaccurately thought to be always of the sweet red variety. (By the same token, gin and dry vermouth was known as Gin and French.) Proportions vary according to individual taste, and many recipes show the gin and vermouth in equal quantities.

2 measures/3 tbsp gin
1 measure/1½ tbsp sweet red vermouth

Add both ingredients to a rocks glass with a couple of ice cubes in it. Stir, and add a twist of lemon rind to garnish.

Bitter Gimlet

This is an old-fashioned aperitif, which could easily be turned into a longer drink by finishing it with chilled tonic or soda water.

1 lime, cut into wedges
1 measure/1½ tbsp gin
2 dashes Angostura bitters

Put the lime into a pitcher and, using a muddler, press the juice out of it. Add the cracked ice, gin and bitters and stir well until chilled. Strain the cocktail into a short tumbler over ice cubes. Add a triangle of lime rind to the drink.

Bartending know-how
The oversized label around each Angostura bitters bottle was an administrative error that just stuck!

Space

... the final frontier? Not quite, but this is a very moreish modern cocktail recipe made with hazelnut liqueur. It makes a good aperitif.

1½ measures/6 tsp gin
1 measure/1½ tbsp Frangelico (or crème de noisette)
½ measure/2 tsp lemon juice

Shake all the ingredients well with ice, and strain into a rocks glass. Add cracked ice and serve.

Bartending know-how
The monk after whom Frangelico is named, and who is credited with its recipe, lived as a hermit in north-west Italy in the 17th century.

Milano

The assertive flavour of Galliano comes through strongly in this short, sour cocktail, which has a long aftertaste.

1 measure/1½ tbsp gin
1 measure/1½ tbsp Galliano
juice of half a lemon

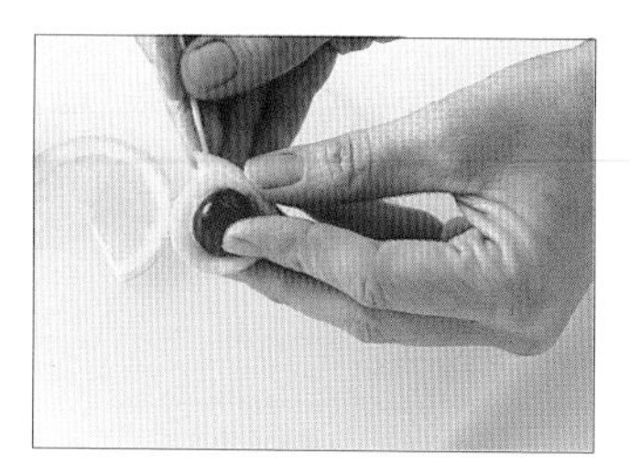

Shake all the ingredients well with ice, and strain into a cocktail glass. Garnish with a cherry and slices of lemon or lime on a cocktail stick.

Oasis

Blue cocktails suddenly became all the rage during the cocktail boom of the 1980s. This is a particularly satisfying mixture that's not too sweet.

2 measures/3 tbsp gin
½ measure/2 tsp blue curaçao
4 measures/6 tbsp tonic water

Pour the gin into a highball glass half-filled with cracked ice. Add the curaçao, top up with the tonic and stir gently. Garnish with a slice of lemon and a sprig of mint.

Bartending know-how
Blue curaçao mixes very well with all clear spirits, giving a striking colour to the cocktail.

Bloodhound

The drink takes its name from the rather gory colour and texture produced by including whole strawberries in the blend.

1½ measures/6 tsp gin
½ measure/2 tsp dry vermouth
½ measure/2 tsp sweet red vermouth
¼ measure/1 tsp crème de fraise
6 strawberries

Put all the ingredients into a liquidizer with ice, and blend for about 20 seconds. Strain into a cocktail glass, and garnish with a final whole strawberry dipped in crème de fraise.

Midsummer Night

The orangey, quinine flavour of Italian Punt e Mes goes well with gin and a modest amount of blackcurrant liqueur in this modern recipe.

1 measure/1½ tbsp gin
1 measure/1½ tbsp Punt e Mes
½ measure/2 tsp crème de cassis

Shake all the ingredients well with ice, and strain into a cocktail glass. You could garnish with a twist of lemon, if you like.

Index

This edition is published by Lorenz Books, an imprint of Anness Publishing Ltd
info@anness.com
www.annesspublishing.com

A CIP catalogue record for this book is available from the British Library.

Publisher: Joanna Lorenz
Editorial Director: Helen Sudell
Photographers: Frank Adam, Steve Baxter & Janine Hosegood
Designer: Nigel Partridge
Production Controller: Ben Worley

DRINK AWARENESS
Always drink responsibly. Do not drink and drive, and avoid alcohol whilst pregnant or trying to conceive.

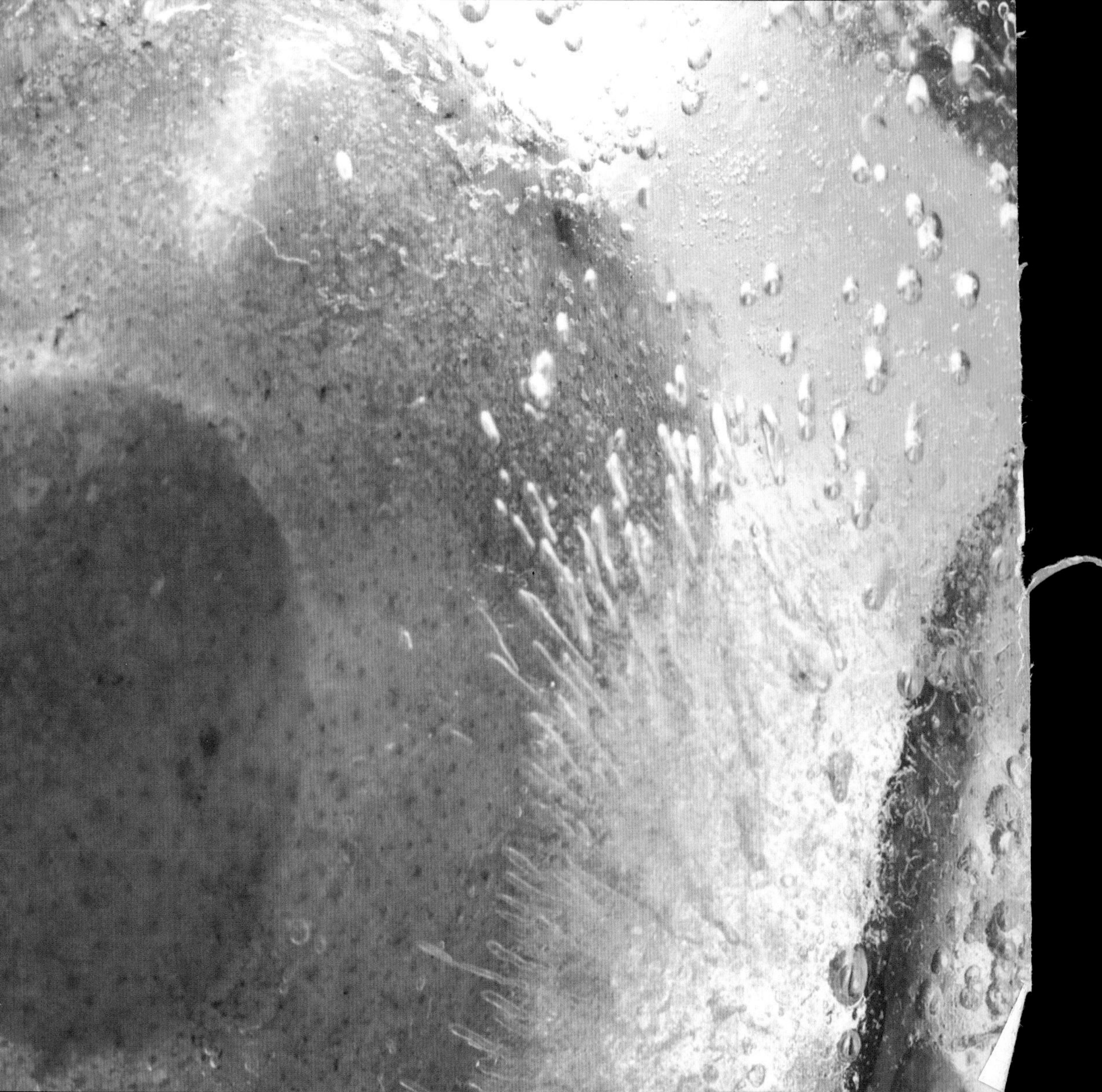